CORNFRY

BY RICH PERIN

Buckman Publishing LLC
est. 2018
1033 Main St. Suite 4
Portland, Oregon 97214

ALIS VOLAT PROPRIIS
SHE FLIES WITH HER OWN WINGS

Congratulations! A **Buckman Publishing** *production is in your hands! We're an unorthodox operation that continues the daredevil tradition of literature, printing new sparks that ignite imagination. Proudly independent,* **Buckman's** *defiant attitude aims to inspire and increase readership in the greater society.*

ALL RIGHTS RESERVED

Words © 2025 Rich Perin
Cover & Book Design:
Ellen Robinette
Fonts used: Garamond,
BEBAS NEUE

ISBN:
9798990017498
LCCN:
2025931955

C.P. Cavafy, "Waiting for the Barbarians", translated by Edmund Keeley & Philip Sherrard, from *Poems for the Millennium*, Jerome Rothenberg & Pierre Joris (Editors), University of California Press © 1995.

Lew Welch, "In Safeway Parking Lots, Old Men Drive Slowly, Backwards", from *Ring of Bone*, City Lights Publishers © 2012.

Ahoy hoy from a trip 'round Portland, Oregon USA!
Find more at **buckmanjournal.com**

Γιατί κ' οι άξιοι ρήτορες δεν έρχονται σαν πάντα
να βγάλουνε τους λόγους τους, να πούνε τα δικά τους;

Γιατί οι βάρβαροι θα φθάσουν σήμερα ·

Why don't our distinguished orators turn up as usual
to make their speeches, say what they have to say?

Because the barbarians are coming today

— C.P. Cavafy, *Waiting for the Barbarians*

CONTENTS

Social Stigma of Singular	07
Cheboygan Shopping Cart Blues	08
Crane City	13
Vito from Buffalo Lives in Portland	14
Burnside Bridge	15
Self Portrait #22	16
The Magic We Make	17
I Come Out Looking Like A Beast	18
Mostly Stomach	19
#43 Debonair	20
The Difference Between Falling Asleep and Passing Out	21
#27 Swap	23
Life is Never as Easy as Two Options	24
Lost Highway	25
Moonless West Texas	26
Austin, Tx	27
The Drag (for the slackers)	28
Karen Finley	30
Lemmings Hold Hands and Have a Grip	31
Tasteless Women on 6th Street	32
Tasteless Men on 6th Street	33
Shop 24 is a Genie Lamp. Give it a Rub	34
Gulf of Mexico	35
Autoimmune Disorder Takes the Wheel	36
#29 Quetzalcoatl	37
William Carlos Williams	38
Contemporary Beat Orphans	39

Esc ape	41
New York City Used To Be Like	42
#35 I Forgot I was a Trickster God and Tricked Myself	43
Jack Kerouac's Liver	44
Rochester	45
Macon Stuck	46
Alcohol	47
Greyhound Blues	49
Self Portrait #41	51
San Francisco	52
Barbary Coast Blues	53
Gertrude Stein	60
Crazy Crows	61
Neal Cassady's Thumb	62
Proxy Waterfall, Oregon Cascades	63
Ken Kesey	64
#30 Lew Welch Wrote A Poem Called "In Safeway Parking Lots, Old Men Drive Slowly. Backwards."	65
Portland	66
Buckman Poem #1	67
History of the Goat Blocks	68
A Sunday Afternoon in Buckman	69
Self Portrait #50	70
Godlike	71
b.lac k sh.eep	72
Index	75

SOCIAL STIGMA OF SINGULAR

You should be allowed to marry yourself
I think

CHEBOYGAN SHOPPING CART BLUES

Gone
myself and shopping cart
gonna roll 48 states
rattling ironweed incantations with
bouquet of hummingbirds for company
we're on the lam for sweetness

I'll work chinatown laundry
lunch on chicken feet
build a stack
arch my back
pick grapes
wheel a load east through californ
easter than salton sea
make wine
tumble deserts
play pickup sticks with cactus needles and
solve the theft of morning dew

Climb mesa of acoma puebla
regard the elder pounding chest
honor the past and its length
remorse the killed and taken

Through colorado rocks I sing loves lost
ramble a harmony for the cliffs
i'll cartwheel like a tambourine
where i stub my toe
plant tomatoes
ozark springs to soak my wheels and feet

Go huck finn
raft the cart
map the hips of mississip and
give delta back its skirt
i'll fish around sunken cypress stumps
leave heads and tails for nesting eagles
it's the proper way to pay respects

Jubilee mobile bay
a flounder fry and crab boil
keep the mosquites far away
plant lavender sprouts on my chest

Me and my cart
tramp astaire
ginger metal rogers
burying treasure all over
a gold tooth
set of dice
kangaroo paw
can of soup
spare char to chew
no national monument will go unblessed
chisel a liking of myself on teddy roosevelt's good
        shoulder
pee on picket fence behind grassy knoll

I'll avoid (new) york city
more spectacle than experience
i praise picklebacks in brooklyn and
taxi rides of ill repute
but times square banned
shopping carts unless gold plated and
a beastie boy is dead

Eat a seagull at every beach to establish scavenging
     rules
in texas you have to eat three grackles
farm a beard in la grange
dance suave with abuelas at san anto flea marts
hunt javelina and smoke wild bacon

In the hill country
long ago when I was cartless
i'll remember lightning breaking horizon
colleen and I by blanco river
pearls in each other's eyes
and when we wandered new orleans
slept like babes on old marigny floor
dreamt of creole treading boards a century before
but those times are gone and haunt like moody spirits
exorcism regret
practice ojo
crack egg into bowl and place it under bed!

Turn tennessee
camp at catfish pond
follow the migration of swifts
derby thru madrugada hue of smokey mounts

Keep north the rolling's good
how flat chicago
king congest of shopping carts
where prairie grass used to wave on lake shore
usurped by dopey concrete order and burning rivers

Don't ask for directions
i've only got mine
i get coffee
watch others socialize flat screens

lazy eyed
all this clicking without knowing what clicks
hens at dispenser
BE-YOCK!

Let us form battalions of shopping carts and not use
    them for shopping
welcome chrome back on the road
quick!
before the kids tattoo shopping carts on their arms and
    chest

I got a different set of expectations wound in
    movement
i prefer the setting sun
waves from china
the float of fireflies
no need of snapshot to prove it

I'll cross into canady
hobo work maple trees
not for the money
solely for the trickle
run along kid caribou
sled my cart
make sleigh
hook strays
go iditarod and have a word with northern lights
keep your dogs far hence!
they see a better life with me

Children will ask if i am santa
santa chains reindeers
santa is heavy and I am long
santa never rolled a day in his life

Gauge my cart on rail tracks
caboose thru fields of wheat and
vacated lines along lost pines
direct to abandoned mines dead of gold
echoes and underground bubbling brook to conversate
maybe get myself a pet billy goat
wool its coat call it junior
make cheese knit sweats
teach dexterities to my hands

Summer upper michigan
lasso mackinac bridge
play harmoni-key
sing a yodel
Good morning, Captain
Good morning to you
I'm the mule skinner
You need down by the old mudline
yah ha aha aha ha ha ha ha
yoda yella heeeee ye heee
ye he he he heeeee
wo hoo hoo ahoo hoo ye he ye he he he

Build a log canoe
big lake island hop
run for mayor of cheboygan
people will call me your honor and I will forget my
        name

Your honor
if i have to die
i'm fine with dying in a ditch as long as coyotes
have at it with my bones and
their pups howl at the belly full moon
until then i'm too beautiful to stand still

CRANE CITY

The bottle cannot be recorked
the bottle is empty
the best man's drooling
the mayor's palming the wrong cheat notes
accountants and lawyers tattooed too
it's squirrel memory operation:
did you forget where you put your nuts do you have nuts
you better get some nuts and put them away

A proclamation of cranes!
teeth in braces hanging forced smiles
one eyed nesting craters

Crane!
circling dumb compass
square assembly
smorgasbord of toothpick bricked

Crane!
high rise cubicle following orders
a mouth cornered no mind to speak its own
don't even have a knee

Crane!
these are not homes!
it's dead smoke mistook as spirit
you're a broom for a wrong witch

VITO FROM BUFFALO LIVES IN PORTLAND

It's his girlfriend's apartment
finding himself with afternoon
sunning on porch
in orange pyjama shorts
rearranges his junk
smokes pot scored from downstairs
neighbor calvin from california who grows
a beard and bingos bitcoins while his wife wiles
behind an insurance desk

Life is a cherry tree and this is spring
tonight vito from buffalo won't be heating a can of
        spaghettios
he's ordering gourmet pizza from her favorite place
a shave sports jacket
pearly white candle lit for two
drink some wine
smoke pot make love and fall asleep
in the morning she'll do dishes before work

If vito offers a horse race tip or
claims to hear an earthquake before it hits
take it

BURNSIDE BRIDGE

Weather sign tells the outside it's 22
the neon shivers
underneath the white stag of burnside bridge
sidewalk stain apparitions of virgin guadalupes and
        mahdi returns
homeless submerged in carpet underlay and
        coughing tarps
winter coats deep off the slab ice ground
in the middle pops jaundice glow of faces coming up
        for air

Where the bridge slow arcs over willamette
where it's too cold to sleep
the river throws snow capped ghosts
slicing ears
the carbonation of soda can't escape before freeze

I sing a song to the bridges
to the flow underneath
the countless river thumbprints
the dance of night and fog
hollering above brave trucks
interstate you flattened tongue!

forehead

right eye   left eye

nose

att emp ted mou sta che

s m i l e

goatee

right shoulder   left shoulder

ruby slipper
heart

stunt rider liver

THE MAGIC WE MAKE

As i look at my breakfast
i notice you and i are no better than bacon
sweating on a skillet
beads of grease appearing like morning dew

When did we become fat and red with burnished rage
threatening each other with oil slicks of anger

A brown frying pan
abandoned in the sink
drowning in sud departed water
a final offering our affair has left
an embarrassment of alchemy
no one is willing to clean

I Come Out Looking Like A Beast

I come out looking like a beast and it didn't take much
hours to get out of bed
find yesterday's shirt
jilt the toothbrush
pan fry chicken thighs
ignore hallway mirror
leave house
where under a shameless sun
the shadow of my hair swarms
my eyes lodge gunny sacks
i smell like chicken
the guy with junk metal shopping cart rolls away
children run to front doors
neighbors peer through cracks and cross themselves
what has portland spat out now
walking the street growling?

Mostly Stomach

This is the tour of the belly
notice tough as guts
go on
give it a punch
no a real punch
follow thru with your shoulder
it can take it
can't do that with the heart
that's another tour
no one goes on that tour anymore
even though it's the cheapest
so throw another
this is the place for fists
get it out of your system

#43 Debonair
(Ex Girlfriendus)

Let's say i'm the one that got away
instead of bandied catch and release trout
let the scouting report last known location
chased into sunset waving satchel of gold
ready to zorro with a rose in his bite

THE DIFFERENCE BETWEEN
FALLING ASLEEP AND PASSING OUT

I go to the railroad tracks late
cast rocks at boxcars of fleeing trains
envy has an arm and dreams of grappling hook

Here comes closing screams
horn in full boar
crossbone lights dancing
iron rails saluting and accounted for
under the bridge ducking the highway
dead car shangri las
sleeping bag sandbars
where old docks used to tie and
the floodplain of the willamette lapped
cobblestone street faded gravestones stuck
with overpass sweat
mostly a scene for deject territorial disputes
my shadow is the only moving sawtooth

Screams get sharper
this locomotive cutter this
locomotive is locomotive!
forget me not!
upon its back and ribs we breathed
from gold rush chinamen
continental divide joiners
dust bowl depression
waving woody guthries and
children of guthries dodging
railyard dick until they
shut the boxcar tight
now it's always going with few getting on

i don't even have the eyes to spot a foothold but
have the sense to wish i did

I launch a stone at empty cargo tank
striking sour gong
final car tap shoes a goodbye
going to moonlight
again without me on it

Leaving the clanks for
pint glass promises chin chinning consolations
i go to the bar where Tad Chi
ate a cookie that was nailed to the wall for two years
sucking 2nd hand nicotine before it got to his lips
facing the beer taps a perfect giant shadow and
i drink it
there is melting
losing the grapple with words i make up words that
echo the spirit

The night dies
i stumble uphill
an obedient engine that could
no fanfare no rocks to throw
back to the apartment that's
quiet as a dead refrigerator
to fathom the difference between
falling asleep and passing out

#27 SWAP
(Ex Girlfriendus)

Did she keep kimonos
the two i gave or
traded at swap party now
someone else wears history

Life is Never as Easy as Two Options

The first involves a buggy drawn by
two horses plodding through fog of
scottish mull acting as if there is no fog

The other features a magician who
uncuffs sleeves and reveals everything
some say it's selfish honesty and reality match

LOST HIGHWAY

The dash lights flicker
the radio dimming
there's thumbing of the dial
preachers screaming in and out
a tumbleweed loose from kansas
bones of last night's fried chicken
lost in the black hole at your feet

Somewhere down the lightless line
a diner waitress offering grits
slinging coffee
dying for a smoke
a chance to slip off shoes
maybe she'll call you hon
ask if you need more butter

How many roads died by interstate
the boa constrictors bring expectations

MOONLESS WEST TEXAS

I walk towards
hangover moon
that's half cut
sometimes
plum by clouds
i show my jaw
stretch neck
toucan mouth
sing in this
swagger because
the shape of
my heart

Lean like
departing flowers

In west texas
when the moon
sets early leaving
disilluminate desert
can't even
see the
ground
steps sink into
airy crackweed sand
a world sewn
shut with
ancient thread

If it wasn't for my breath
i wouldn't be anywhere

she came to town young looking for a career outside disillusioned college plan and decided on private investigator a hero hunting down deadbeat dads and didn't want to do traditional route of police or military service so applied for a repo man position because she would learn skip tracing how to find someone who doesn't want to be found and got giddy because she likes to spy but the timing belt of her car snapped and her boyfriend kept driving and fucked it up she went back home a couple of years ago changed for the better

THE DRAG (FOR THE SLACKERS)
Guadalupe Street, Austin, TX

Hi, how are you?
botoxed lost wrinkles no grime
guadalupe was an old deck of cards in cowboy hands
shuffle and reshuffle droop edged
oily brown gloss from worry
just enough defibrillator for loser gamblers
it was down
sure weren't pretty
but it had a pulse and a sense of it

Then fat bucks took a seat at the table
spreading sterile
a great antimicrobial clean
surgical grade scrubbers in mindless wash
those fortunate to make a mark too often reveal how
    unimaginative they are
all the way to horizons spackle and glue holds
the old two floor record store split into
coffeehouse chain franchise and chain franchise noodle
house which is next to the franchise chain bagel shop
which is next to clothing chain franchise next to bank
too big to fail
now the only wail is jamba juice and five dollar taco

Where are the heavy coughing bumming for change?
the guy making a living throat singing?
the hippie selling gen u EINE new mexica crystals?
street gal making handmade macramé while you wait?
someone off their meds dealing dollar-a-pop tarot and
    sees the future clearly?
where are the thieving punks?

From east texas double wide bayous
deserts and gulf coast flats
blanks from dallas and houston suburbs seeking
    character
kids came keen with big eyes for wrinkles and grime
without the blind of phones and gps
do the police even patrol here anymore?
and for godsake where is the smell?
and where is the guy throat singing for change?

KAREN FINLEY

Is it drowning
is it birth
there's reason why rhythm
holds urgency

Questions grow louder
when answers don't add
look at what's breathed
a voice scrambling for oxygen
the wise renouncing reality

LEMMINGS HOLD HANDS AND HAVE A GRIP

It's not like we are doing anything new
mayans gutted from pyramids
zealot picnics at stoning or stake burning
someone led a cheer and everyone complied

There's repetition in our blood
herds following the biggest horns
there's no charity in the obvious
what is it about cliffs that make us think we can fly?

TASTELESS WOMEN ON 6TH STREET

There's tasteless women on 6th street and
i can't eat them

They laugh feedback
conveniently vacuum sealed
wear 40 coats of paint and
talk like parrots on speed

Their breasts are barbie doll flesh
large balls of man made anti gravity
they walk upright because
their heads are lighter than air

There's tasteless women on 6th street and
i won't eat them

TASTELESS MEN ON 6TH STREET

They'd beat the sweet
bejesus out of you
if they didn't
have a gun
even
then

SHOP 24 IS A GENIE LAMP. GIVE IT A RUB
24 hour convenience store, 6th street, Austin, Texas

The ceiling lights ring nonstop
compressors throat chant
fresh five gallon suds bucket
burned by ammonia fights
greasy jojos stung under
mad glare heat lamps
the restroom never in
order is doing a favor
the wall in the alley
once bounced the clack of 3am dice and
took six john wesley hardin bullets

Beyond the souvenir t-shirts and
flip flops with texas declarations of size
in the aisle where santería
candles and chicharrónes meet
el borracho claims two cans of clamato
walks to the register grabs bouquet of last chance roses
wires oaxaca and buys a pack of electric guitar strings

GULF OF MEXICO

Oh gulf of mexico
how i wish you were whiskey and
love that does not wash away

But you are a poor man's beer
awash with old spit malt
raking long regrets

I am a blue jellyfish
stranded on the beach
bloated with salty ghosts

Mortality, making its presence known, a brood of sledgehammer heads magnetized to bone, from cranium, steeling the neck, shoulders, spine, hips, fixing brace on legs, burdened. Sledgehammer heads wonder why they are not slamming because that is their purpose, so they wait impatient and ring. They don't figure bone is not a handle. Sledgehammer heads go Sunday cathedral and the only thing that kills the carillon is a dose of morphine.

Administration of one dose of morphine costs twenty
two hundred dollars at the emergency room.

I have broad shoulders. So did Goliath. When I am in a hospital bed twisting to the contortions of weighted bone, throat fraying, visionary pain just before morphine drip, I smell the glue factory, I learn the surprise of mortality, appreciate Goliath's last thought after he got hit between the eyes.

#29 QUETZALCOATL
(Ex Girlfriendus)

I will be mentioned in the future
a sidenote perhaps something like
"i had a boyfriend who drove a big old
cadillac and it was a smooth ride"

Does casual reference draw a smile
a glint from surprise re-emergence
of easy dissolved memory
now sleight of hand sneaking back in

I am history so i don't know
i suspect a smile i hope a smile
it can be tinged with regret too
just enough to comfort my pride

WILLIAM CARLOS WILLIAMS

Hey doctor
i see wheelbarrows everywhere
not just red ones too

Consequences rise and die like rabbits
from boundless to bound
snail finding its corner

CONTEMPORARY BEAT ORPHANS

Up-against-the-wall monstertrucker city
nitro nerved and junkdog plagued
eager sphincter machines
reciting telemarketing scripts outside work
video game hunchbacks with lard fingertips
boasting ranks of shotgun halo

Rage thumps thumps thumps meathook foreheads
streets with tabloid congeniality
a dodgy swarm of gimcrack
birds of parasites
cubic zirconia eyed
crude fratboy fatgirl joke philosophy
a giant scrum of brutes and brutettes
"and somebody's giving booze to these
goddamn things!
It won't be long before they tear us to shreds
Jesus, look at the floor!
Have you ever seen so much blood?"

What lives on the killing floor?
what grows?
what digs with roots and comes up trumps?
why does halo look like cathrine wheel?
why so many judas cows?

Contemporary beat orphans!
feeling no joy from tattoos and redbull
can mouth do more than bite and chew?
feet more than lines and cues?
digitals corrals
all accomplice

grifters grifting and grifted
the dream without dare
slumber
the dare dead

Contemporary beat orphans!
go fabulous roman candles
burn skull drudgery
evaporate yawns
find sunflower and hold tight

Not unhinged. More so. Born without a hinge. No possibility of a door. Jointless. That's what we are dealing with. Everywhere.

I stress there isn't an impression of anything like a jumping castle. Certainly spineless, yes. But lots of cartilage. There's no fun bouncing on knuckles.

There's a little bit of meat. The wrong muscle. A gym membership strength. Plenty of cartilage, though. No shortage of cartilage. And lotion.

That's the tide of things. That's the swim. Breathing through reeds submerged. Riding a friendly gang of ocean going turtles. Island hopping. Safe houses. Incognito the way to go. Standing out in a school of fish, highbeaming the shadows, declarations of presence, natural selection eventually arrives to make the obvious adjudication.

Until then, inconspicuousness. Indiscretion. While doing a complete 180. Hiding the hinge so to speak. Don't be caught with one. Until the right moment. Then bam! They won't know what they're missing.

New York City Used To Be Like

Nonchalant old men snapping car antennas
to measure their bocce balls in queens

#35 I Forgot I was a Trickster God and Tricked Myself
(Ex Girlfriendus)

I forgot I was a trickster god and tricked myself. That's what happens when tricksters forget. This is how fools are made. I forget often. The bale of wool charged through the barbed wire leaving snagged wisps. This happened a year ago. The wisps are tattooed by rust and mudded from yesterday's rain. Even languid little flags wave to draw attention.

JACK KEROUAC'S LIVER

This bar walks into a drunk
it never stood a chance
sauntered in dandy
bottled to the teeth
flushed with barrels of confidence
realizes too late it's short stacked
sweet jesus!
only one bar supply to satisfy
    shore leave
      merchant marine
        leading with
          niagara swig!

Some people wear their
armor on the inside
steeled for fights between reflections
a factory of foils tempered with sour mash
some people drown
grow gills then
refuse to breath

Oh québécois!
that liver of yours
was slingshot that did sling thou and deliver
the price holed your soul
but there
before gut rot
the great unrestraint leap of
    bluebird in high lullaby
      cooing for diner waitress

ROCHESTER

It was easy to drink lots of beer
it made outside bearable

After eating the garbage plate at Nick Tahou's
i returned to the interpretation of an irish pub
stole one of their red upholstered chairs
drove it back to oregon via texas in my minivan
it's what i am sitting on right now

MACON STUCK

I wish i could
say the distant foghorn was
a harbored merchant ship
but it's a cargo train
shut steel traps empty of drifters
gravel and ammonia full
choleric wheels inhaling then
leaving loose teeth
fantail of colorsucking dust

Ribs arteries and spine
for the city that sags in heat
decidedly landlocked
a train heels between the lines
a ship is big as an ocean

ALCOHOL

Alcohol
oh alcohol!
mad saint revelator running thru my liver
rescuing me from mediocrity

I remember the good ol' days
drunk in australia
where I loved liquor so much I became bartender
invented cocktails
mastered martinis
pranks with lush comrades
          we'd go to parking lots
          lift and carry volkswagen beetles to different
          parking lots
where I danced on stage with the violent femmes and
          promptly thrown off stage
where I wrote on bathroom walls the alcoholic
          philosophy of friedrich nietzsche: "alcohol
          kills brain cells but only the weak ones!"
where I would sit in university lectures loaded on rum
          even though I wasn't a student
where I would karaoke and instead of singing I'd recite
          poetry

After drinking through australia I drank to america
sneaking a flask of canadian whiskey onto the staten
          island ferry getting hammered while statue of
          liberty floated by
got drunk in denver with a poet who had no teeth
          and I couldn't understand a word he said
got drunk at the electric lounge in austin where they
          sold lonestar beer for a buck twenty five and I

47

got up on stage slurrrrrrrrrrrring through a
poem like a poet from denver who had no
teeth
in tucson arizona keanu reeves bought me a beer and
I was going to ask him if he starred in any
good movies besides bill and ted's excellent
adventure but he bought me a beer and I
didn't want to show any disrespect
in san diego after a tequila frenzy I went skinny dipping
under a full moon with a gal named june
at niagara falls with two friends and a guitar we sang
bob dylan tunes while brown bagging a bottle
of old crow and later I kissed a gal from new
hampshire

But this is not alcoholics victorious
how many hangovers waking the next day my head
a split hard boiled egg and tongue an old
man armpit?
how many shirts carrying beer stain shroud of turin?
how many times in strange dark bars trying to impress
strange beautiful women with phoniness and
terrible drunk poetry?
how many times asking myself "did I really spend fifty
bucks on beer last night?"
when it takes ten beers to buzz
when a stomach reveals for the gutter
when the soul dissolves
froth of disgruntlement overflows!

Alcohol
oh alcohol!
mad saint revelator running thru my liver
rescuing me from mediocrity

GREYHOUND BLUES

Thirty two hours from san francisco
my one legged sister is faster than this bus
somber eyed driver sits like buddha
hopes of heavy foot get stuck with pickups and
     dropoffs
kerrville sonora ozona fort stockton
van horn after dawn
momentum chopped since sass of san antone
relentless west texas
where division of distance and time cruelly counts

Thirty two hours from san francisco
fresh parolee from state pen
     searching plastic bag corners and jacket pockets
     fishing coins for truck stop chicken
across the aisle junkies younger than they look snore
     in harmony with teeth out
four rows down hanging feet more holes than sock
     happy to have a bed

My one legged sister is faster than this bus
latrine door don't close right
no one bothers to solve it
we're highway doped and all sapped
tinted windows bruise and catch smudge of hair and
     face

Old man bible thumper says he's memorized book of
     proverbs
says this here is just like the land of nod
oaxaca farmhand listens but doesn't know english
low brimmed owl and quiet

Chance rides in the west
anticipation unbundles twigs of nerves
patience is a club
how long before the end of the continent
where the sun tucks
last in the world to sing a lullaby goodnight
thirty two hours from san francisco
my one legged sister is faster than this bus

SELF PORTRAIT #41
Sometimes I Feel Like the Last One Standing

Hare there or salamander trickling down granite face washed up whale hong kong mountain if i am not by myself people say let's keep moving i want to stay at the huckleberry and draw its portrait or elsewhere i'll pick up fallen arm of joshua tree and take it back with me it's just a mirror or tail i forgot

SAN FRANCISCO

Under the japanese ink
    moon scene taxi driver takes
       a loop from upper haight behind lombard
   charges down grades sucks in
  the gut at leveled intersections lands with
 thud bounces back to teethed descent
  repeating until the thick of chinatown
    everything in san francisco is suspension

Parallel parks without fuss of turning his neck
walks into the last north beach bar where a saloon
    piano plays
holding a brown paper bag that would seem
    unimportant if not for strong clutch even after
    eight pints and conversations with out-of-towners
    who don't know what they've stumbled into
gripped

BARBARY COAST BLUES
San Francisco

1

california street
   hips under
      limbo stick
paved over drop jaw
a burial
      mound of opium drool
      rum swindles
         vigilance committee ropes and
            earthquake ash

2

      cable cars
   saved by tourists
everyone is here now
   then some more
been
   like that for
      thirty years

3

all succumb
camera eyed
framed

4

office workers are
　　a breed and
　　　rule the
　　　　world
　　　　even
　　　　　in
　　　　absence

5

the flight and haunting
low corona bleeds highrise edge

6

chinatown
brass belt buckled
　　old leather

7

stockton street
tubs of knotted
　　root vegetables and
　　　dried seafood
　　plod the
　air

8

    grapes on
       sale
 dollar a pound
tiny grandmas peck and
   drop overripe and bruised
 leaving
    only the best
sidewalks
  sticked in
    grape juice skin

9

more grandmas
turning nectarines
poking gooseberries
questioning fish bladder

10

bathtub laundry
      old scandals from
   third story
  windows

11

coffeebean
  shuck in
    verdigris awning
     watching
   colombus avenue
  mummified

12

bar doors
  left open calling
    fruit flies to
    dither

13

where
 bathrooms
    haven't changed since 1952
down
    switchback
        wooden stairs that
      wince
 to basement
how do they clean it?
how do they stand?

14

if kerouac were
  alive he'd be
    117

15

vallejo
    gardens
        saluting
            bay bridge
millionaire
    rows
    killed all crows

16

the natural recline of hillsides
    offer relax
        content
            elbow on
            sidestreet
            curb with
            joint or 40
if you can't
    sit on a curb with
        vice then you're
            no longer
                in san francisco

17

tadich grill gents
    serve chowder
        in long white
            linen and gloved
oysters rockefeller

18

transamerica pyramid
    old
  newsprint
    denture
brutal syringe

19

handlebar
  mustache
  afternoon

20

for having
    bird brains
pigeons
    sure
      are
        restless

21

this was mud
  where
    brine shrimp
      spurt
    seaman and
      eggs
now bankers and
obligations

21

little italy
dead garlic

23

every language
  is heard
  in san
    francisco
but not
  sailors

24

jack kerouac lane
19 cans of vienna sausage

fine wine sometimes bandit on fire running with
hands up hands up but no surrender. a swan dive
temper. blacksmiths drink wine with no hands.

CRAZY CROWS

Candalibre
Counterlivre
Candelabra
Cantilever

NEAL CASSADY'S THUMB

I've been licked
greased a few dollar bills
left my print plenty on what goes 'round
twirled sledgehammers
juggling is art of momentum

A holy thumb
stopped a thousand cars
tapped dents into steering wheels
at the end of the pool cue aiming weight
a lighthouse in jazz cellars
director over a lover's thigh
was sucked on until i was two

PROXY WATERFALL, OREGON CASCADES
For Amelia

old recluse opens sluice
spills slurry of stars that
swells the verdant deep
dashes under drunk trees and
disembarrass rocks that
nurse hatching mermaids
after tending wild ginger
shooting a huckleberry or two
before a river can say too much
slips like a grabbed fish down a lava tube

KEN KESEY

Hey farmer!
you are in heaven
aligning the stampede
a ye! a ya!
and look here you have a whip now
running alongside
that camaraderie
feel that
the best witness is in it

#30 Lew Welch Wrote A Poem Called
    "In Safeway Parking Lots,
    Old Men Drive Slowly.
    Backwards."
    (Ex Girlfriendus)

I drive the underground safeway parking lot
do a lap or two windows down and yodel
the hollow longs for more than
tire squeeze and car alarm set

I get serious and park
consider the walls and defying beams
then sing with weights of echoes
letting the resonance of architecture carry the load

PORTLAND

Between the muttonchops hangs
a smile that wasn't there in the
midwest where it was hidden by
tater tot casserole and snow
neither was the electric dyed
hair bravado of rain in knit work
guile of backstreet getaways or
eyes that looked up

Freeway escaped in dead grandma's
old sedan with nothing but inklings
thirsting for juice seeking cross
pollinating vines that refuse strip mall
theories and expectations dwindled down
to routines replanted at converging rivers
now he's playing ping pong on a table found
free on a street

BUCKMAN POEM #1
neighborhood philosophy

Free
to make
mistakes
but quickly
recognizing
them before
repetition
loops like
a python

HISTORY OF THE GOAT BLOCKS
(SE 11th and Belmont, Portland, Oregon)

Before cost efficient architecture tombstoned
    the goat blocks
before goats grazed the empty lot
before old produce warehouses and bar monte carlo
    disintegrated in flames
before belmont street car and speakeasies and dice
    games and faro and sailors
before little lake was drained and cuts of doug fir and
    pokes of stumps
before city of east portland and cyrus buckman's
    apple orchard
before wagon trails mule skinners and astoria pelt
before lewis and clark and europeans that never bathed
when twelve pound steelhead were easy as a grab
berries and camas plenty
when people were of the land and honored
    subduction zones
ever since the ice dam broke
everything has always been coming here

A Sunday Afternoon in Buckman

They are out sunning eyelashes
laughing like lavender
swinging hands of uptick
in the afternoon that doesn't feel used

forehead

right eye   left eye

nose
moustache gray

s m i l e
goatee gray

right shoulder   left shoulder

lung wings   lung wings

c/s

*

* the liver is the only organ that regenerates

I don't feel old. I do feel used. A good life has innumerable unknowns. It never gets old.

#

Living through it is not enough. Understanding it is.

#

The audacity to contemplate existence. It stumps me too much. Amazement is good but that's not the destination. I've roosted on a strange perch. I wish I could share these things with someone else.

B.LAC K   SH.EEP

You busted out spokes
flung from circumference
flying without hub
the air is faint and failing in vigor
pockets filled with rocks and lumps
a mope needing the honest flight of arrows

The wheel's stern like a coffin lid
its habit to crush and return the fold
the choir sings same note
congregation of discourageous bouillabaisse never
    to marry stir of spoon
woe to nonplussed!
when it moves it soon
    reaches uncomfortableness then
    retreats nonplussed
who wants to congeal in that fat and
    make that gravity?

You who gather will wander
    skip nets
    detach lures
    shrug lapel grabs
    escape pyramid booby traps
    carry the smarts to take two shots to
        establish triangulation
no brick on leash
more like a hooptie tuned to navajo radio
    determined to prove curvature of earth
dodging wing clippers and shoulder curlers
no slipstream congratulating onward
all headwinds less than thankless
you who are unwant

There is no need to unite
no call to form a flying wedge heralding a new era
a resolute hope you remain in the raffle and never
    suffer the pick
when you don't know what's funny anymore and
    only crows and cats hear your voice
when you awake and someone built a moat
recount exaltations
let roar from your cave
the valley will mistake it for supersonic jet or
    condo excavations
the daring rogue rimbaud
better to die a moving soul
a tip of the hat and
top of the morning to your secret hardihood

INDEX

Cheboygan Shopping Cart Blues

salton sea: unintentional man-made salt lake in southeast California that is slowly evaporating.

acoma puebla: (pueblo) oldest continually inhabited place in North America.

Jubilee mobile bay/a flounder fry and crab boil.... Jubilee in Mobile Bay is a weather event that causes sea life to rise to the surface and towards the shore allowing people to grab an easy catch. Communal cookouts on the beach are common.

tramp astaire/ ginger metal rogers: Fred Astaire and Ginger Rogers, Hollywood golden era dance duo.

grassy knoll: Dealy Plaza, Dallas. Rumored position of sniper that assassinated JFK.

picklebacks: a shot of pickle juice.

beastie boy(s): NYC hip hop group.

javelina: wild boar.

marigny: New Orleans neighborhood.

ojo: folk magic, Mexico.

madrugada: the blue luminosity before dawn.

iditarod: dog sled race in Alaska

keep your dogs far hence!

—*The Waste Land*, T.S. Eliot.

yodel from *Mule Skinner Blues*, traditional.

cheboygan: town in Michigan.

Burnside Bridge

Downtown bridge that crosses over the Willamette river, I-5, and Union Pacific railroad.

white stag of burnside bridge.... 1940s neon sign featuring a deer, Portland historical landmark.

The Difference Between
Falling Asleep and Passing Out

willamette: Willamette river that runs through Portland.
locomotive is locomotive!
forget me not!
—*Sunflower Sutra*, Allen Ginsberg.
i go to the bar where…. Basement Pub, once known as
    Portland's smokiest dive.
Tad Chi: Portland old-timer, relic

The Drag

The stretch of retail and recreation that runs along Guadalupe
    Street, the western border of the University of Texas,
    Austin. Long history of counterculture.
Hi, how are you?…. Message of iconic frog graffiti (Jeremiah
    The Innocent) by songwriter Daniel Johnson (and
    popularized by Kurt Cobain) that is located on Guadalupe
    and 21st.

Karen Finley

Performer, artist, one of the NEA Four (National Endowment
    of the Arts) whose proposed grants were vetoed due to
    conservative political pressure.

Tasteless Women on 6th Street

6th Street, Austin, Texas, entertainment district where the street
    is closed to vehicles on weekend nights.

Shop 24

john wesley hardin: 19th century outlaw.
chicharrónes: fried pork skin.

Autoimmune Disorder Takes the Wheel

carillon: set of bells in a bell tower.

#29 Quetzalcoatl

Feathered-serpent deity from Mesoamerica.

William Carlos Williams

Poet who wrote *The Red Wheelbarrow*.

Contemporary Beat Orphans

"and somebody's giving booze to these goddamn things...."
—Hunter S. Thompson, *Fear and Loathing in Las Vegas*.
catherine wheel: medieval torture device.
fabulous roman candles
—*On the Road*, Jack Kerouac.

Rochester

Nick Tahou's: Nick Tahou's Tots, diner that invented the garbage plate in 1918: baked beans, macaroni salad, home fries, french fries, mustard, ketchup, and choice of meat (hamburger, hot dog, gristle, etc.).

Alcohol

violent femmes: American musical act.

San Francisco

walks into the last north beach bar.... Specs' Twelve Adler Museum Café.

Barbary Coast Blues

Before the land reclamation that became San Francisco's
    Financial District, once was the bay shoreline known as
    the Barbary Coast, a rowdy precinct of bars, dance halls,
    gambling dens, and cheap lodgings. Area of high vice.

tadich grill: California's oldest restaurant.
transamerica pyramid: Modernist 1972 skyscraper, tallest in the
    city until 2018, when another financial district skyscraper
    was completed.

Buckman Poem #1

Inner-southeast Portland neighborhood

History of the Goat Blocks

muleskinner: person who marshals horses/mules/donkeys
    that plough irrigation channels.

Self Portrait #50

c/s: con safos, Chicano term often tagged in mural or graffiti,
    roughly implying, "Can't touch this, it is all heart."

b.lac k   sh.eep

bouillabaisse: fish soup
hooptie: old, beat up, used car that often has a large engine.
daring rouge rimbaud: Arthur Rimbaud, an instigator of
    modern poetry who stopped writing at 20.

www.ingramcontent.com/pod-product-compliance
Lightning Source LLC
Chambersburg PA
CBHW020816130626
46554CB00006B/2474